Original title:
Through the Heart's Eyes

Author: Dorian Ashford
ISBN HARDBACK: 978-9916-88-844-5
ISBN PAPERBACK: 978-9916-88-845-2

Embracing Vulnerability's Sight

In shadows we often hide,
Fearing what lies within.
But there's strength in our tears,
A light to let love in.

Let walls begin to fall,
And hearts start to reveal.
For in the rawest truth,
Connection, we shall feel.

Windows to Innermost Feelings

Eyes, a canvas so clear,
Painting dreams and our fears.
Every glance a story told,
In silence, the heart speaks near.

With each heartbeat we share,
A window swung open wide.
Inviting the world inside,
Where our souls can reside.

Light Beneath the Surface

Beneath the calm exterior,
A tempest gently churns.
The depth of hidden tides,
Where passion often burns.

Seek the glow within us,
Where true colors are found.
In darkness and in light,
Love's echo will surround.

Heartstrings and Twilight Colors

As twilight paints the sky,
Heartstrings begin to sway.
Each note a soft caress,
In the dusk's gentle play.

Melodies of the night,
In whispers, they entwine.
With every hue that fades,
Our spirits intertwine.

A Glimpse Within the Pulse

In whispers soft the heartbeats sigh,
A dance of shadows, a fleeting cry.
Beneath the skin, the rhythm flows,
Secrets deep where no one knows.

Echoes linger in silent nights,
Fleeting dreams in gentle flights.
Within the pulse, the stories dwell,
A world unseen, a hidden shell.

Seeking Truth in Every Beat

Each pulse a question, each thrum a quest,
In the search for answers, we rarely rest.
Through tidal waves of doubt and fear,
We delve deeper, holding dear.

The cadence tells of joys and pains,
In every cycle, what remains?
A journey long, a path unknown,
Within the beats, the truth be shown.

Portraits of Passion's Glow

Colors swirl in heartbeat's light,
Wisps of love that shine so bright.
Brush strokes soft on canvas wide,
Emotions captured, can't be denied.

Each pulse a brush, each beat a hue,
Creating visions, fresh and true.
In every portrait, stories sing,
Of passion's dance, of life's own spring.

The Depths of Sentiment

In caverns deep where feelings grow,
The heart's own lanterns softly glow.
Echoes of laughter, whispers of tears,
Mapping the journey through all the years.

In rich textures of pain and bliss,
Love's essence wrapped in a quiet kiss.
The deeper you dive, the more you see,
In the depths of sentiment, you'll find me.

Navigating the Currents of Desire

In shadows deep, we often glide,
Yearning hearts where secrets hide.
Waves of longing ebb and flow,
Guiding us where passions grow.

A flicker here, a glance that stings,
Unraveled dreams, sweet whispers bring.
In every sigh a story spun,
A dance of souls, just begun.

Quiet Revelations in Color

Soft hues brush against the night,
Whispers of dawn, a gentle light.
In quiet corners, colors blend,
Creating paths where thoughts transcend.

Emerald leaves, cerulean skies,
In solitude, our spirit flies.
From silence, beauty starts to gleam,
Painting moments, woven dream.

The Allure of Unfelt Touch

A ghostly hand, a fleeting trace,
Yearning hearts in empty space.
Lingering words, unspoken calls,
In stillness, every silence falls.

Echoes dance on muted air,
A heart entwined in deep despair.
What could be in shadows lost,
The weight of love, the heavy cost.

Landscapes of Emotional Landscapes

Mountains rise where sorrows dwell,
Oceans deep where feelings swell.
Rivers flow through valleys dim,
Trails of hope on pathways slim.

Each sunset brings a brand new start,
Painting hues upon the heart.
In every tear, a lesson learned,
In landscapes vast, our spirits burned.

The Beauty in Gentle Glances

In silent moments, soft and slow,
A glance can spark a secret glow.
Each fleeting look, a world untold,
In love's embrace, hearts brave and bold.

With just a twinkle, the night ignites,
Reflecting dreams beneath the lights.
A gaze that lingers, pure and true,
In silence speaks what words undo.

Reflective Hues of Desire

In twilight's kiss, colors collide,
With every shade, passion's tide.
A canvas painted with longing sighs,
Where hearts unveil their muted cries.

Every brushstroke, a stolen glance,
Lost in a moment, a fleeting chance.
With hues of hope, and shadows near,
Desire whispers, sweet and clear.

The Echo of a Warm Embrace

In the quiet after, silence hums,
A heartbeat's echo softly comes.
Wrapped in warmth, two souls align,
As time slips by, divine, benign.

A tender hug, a timeless spell,
Where whispers linger, hearts can dwell.
In every squeeze, love finds a space,
Resonating in a gentle grace.

Secrets Lost in Time's Tenderness

In shadows deep, where memories fade,
Secrets linger in the time-worn shade.
Whispers travel through the years,
In tender hearts, they hold our fears.

With gentle hands, we trace the lines,
Of faded stories, love defines.
Past echoes linger, softly chime,
In hushed confessions, lost in time.

The Glow of Tender Memories

In the stillness of the night,
Whispers of love take flight.
Soft echoes of laughter ring,
In the warmth that memories bring.

Faded photographs we hold,
Tales of youth and dreams retold.
Every smile, a cherished flame,
Igniting hearts, forever the same.

Time may pass, but never fade,
The bonds that life has made.
In shadows of our yesterdays,
Tender remnants gently blaze.

As twilight paints the sky,
We remember those who fly.
In our hearts, a glowing spark,
Guides us through the endless dark.

An Ode to Unseen Connections

Beneath the surface, currents flow,
Unseen threads that gently grow.
In a glance or fleeting sigh,
A world of feeling passing by.

Hands outstretched in silent prayer,
An understanding, pure and rare.
Though we wander far apart,
Echoes bind the hidden heart.

With every step, each whispered word,
Souls entwined, though not inferred.
Across the miles, our dreams align,
In the quiet, your heart is mine.

Together we rise, though apart we stand,
An unbroken bond, hand in hand.
In the dance of fate we trust,
Our spirits united, bright and just.

Flickers of Forgotten Dreams

In the attic, shadows creep,
Faded visions start to weep.
Once ablaze with hope and fire,
Now they linger, lost desire.

Ghosts of dreams we laid to rest,
Whisper softly, "We were blessed."
In twilight's grasp, they softly gleam,
Flickers of our lost esteem.

What once was clear, now fades to gray,
Yet in our hearts they choose to stay.
A gentle pull from long ago,
Reminds us all that we let go.

So let us rise to greet the clear,
Embrace the past, hold dreams sincere.
For in the darkness, sparks remain,
To light the path through joy and pain.

The Horizon of Heartfelt Moments

As dawn awakens, colors merge,
From the depths, our spirits surge.
Every heartbeat, a simple song,
Uniting souls where we belong.

Across the sky, a canvas bright,
Moments shared, pure delight.
In laughter's echo, we find our place,
A tapestry of love and grace.

When shadows fall and dreams take flight,
Hearts entwined in soft twilight.
With every glance, a story unfolds,
In tender whispers, love consoles.

The horizon calls, we heed its song,
In every moment, we grow strong.
Hand in hand, we face the dawn,
In the embrace of love, we are reborn.

Dreamscapes of Intimate Truth

In twilight whispers, shadows dance,
As secrets drift in every chance.
Beneath the stars, our spirits merge,
In dreams, we find the sacred urge.

The heart's soft murmurs, softly tread,
Entwined in hopes, where none have fled.
Through velvet nights, we chase the light,
In dreamscapes, we reclaim our flight.

The Light of Lost Moments

Fleeting glimmers, memories cast,
In golden hues, they fade so fast.
A laughter shared, a tear's embrace,
In every glance, we find our place.

Through windows wide, the past unfurls,
In light of dusk, our story swirls.
Each moment held, a timeless thread,
In heart's tapestry, forever spread.

The Ink of Memory's Quill

In scribbled notes, our tales reside,
With every stroke, we learn to glide.
Time's ink flows thick on parchment's face,
Recording love, our fervent grace.

Beneath the moon, our thoughts take flight,
Crafted in shadows, brushed with light.
Pages turn, yet still we cling,
To whispered dreams, and songs we sing.

Interludes of Infinite Ideas

In quiet moments, we explore,
A world of thoughts, forevermore.
Like scattered stars in endless night,
Each spark ignites with pure delight.

From whispered hopes to dreams profound,
In interludes, our truths are found.
With open minds, we brave the quest,
Unraveling the heart's request.

The Soul's Gentle Palette

In hues of dusk, the heart does play,
Soft whispers of the fading day.
Each shade a memory, bright and bold,
Painted stories waiting to be told.

With every stroke, an echo sings,
Crafting joy from fragile things.
The canvas breathes, a quiet sigh,
As colors dance beneath the sky.

The Warmth of Shared Silence

In moments still, our spirits meet,
A quiet bond, a gentle heat.
No words are needed, just a glance,
In silence deep, we find our dance.

The world may whirl in endless sound,
Yet here, in peace, true love is found.
With hearts aligned, we softly glow,
In this embrace, the silence flows.

Imprints of Love's Journey

Each footstep marks the path we've made,
In laughter shared, in fears displayed.
A tapestry of days gone by,
Woven tight, we cannot lie.

Through storms and suns, our story grows,
In each small act, our love just shows.
A fragrant trail of dreams and tears,
The road ahead, beyond our years.

Threads of Thought in Twilight

As daylight fades, reflections shine,
In twilight's grasp, our thoughts entwine.
Each thread a dream, a hope, a fear,
In quiet minds, the truth draws near.

With every breath, the night reveals,
The heart's soft tempo, how it feels.
In shadows cast, our visions flare,
Threads of thought weave the evening air.

The Subtlety of a Sigh

A breath escapes, soft and light,
Fleeting moments shrouded in night.
Words unspoken linger in air,
In the silence, my heart lays bare.

With every sigh, a story unfolds,
Of love and loss, of dreams untold.
A gentle wave against my soul,
In that quiet, I feel whole.

The weight of longing heavy yet brief,
Each inhale dances with disbelief.
In whispers, our souls collide,
In the subtlety of a sigh, we confide.

The language of hearts, simple yet grand,
In the space between, we understand.
Connections woven without a sound,
In the silence, true love is found.

Heartbeats in Whispers

In the shadows, soft beats align,
Silent rhythms, our hearts entwine.
Each pulse a secret, a tender embrace,
In whispered moments, we find our place.

Through the noise of the world, we hear,
The quiet thrum that draws us near.
In every heartbeat, a promise is spun,
In these whispers, we become one.

Fleeting echoes in the dark,
Light as feathers, igniting a spark.
Underneath the stars, silence prevails,
Heartbeats whisper where love never fails.

With every thud, a tale unfolds,
In hushed tones, our destiny holds.
Together we linger, lost in the sound,
In heartbeats, our truth is found.

A Tidal Wave of Emotions

High tides surge under moon's glowing light,
Waves crashing down, fierce and bright.
Feelings rise like the ocean's tide,
In this chaos, we won't hide.

Rollercoaster highs, and deep lows,
Where the river of passion freely flows.
Each swell a journey, it pulls, it breaks,
In the depths, our heartache wakes.

Caught in the currents, we drift and sway,
Lost in the rush, we're whisked away.
Against the shore, our dreams collide,
In this tidal wave, we won't divide.

With every ebb, a new dawn breaks,
On the horizon, each moment shakes.
Through storms and calm, we learn, we grow,
In the tidal wave, our love will flow.

Glances that Speak Volumes

A fleeting look, sharp and divine,
In that moment, our hearts align.
No words exchanged, yet we both know,
In a glance, our feelings flow.

Eyes that shimmer like the stars,
Telling stories of our scars.
In silence, we dance, our souls in flight,
Glances whisper truths wrapped in light.

Each meeting of gazes, a universe found,
In that instant, no need for sound.
In soft awareness, we share our dreams,
Through glances that unravel at the seams.

The depth of love in every stare,
A bond unspoken, precious and rare.
In the quiet warmth, we evolve,
In glances that speak, our hearts resolve.

The Symphony of Silent Words

In twilight's hue, whispers play,
Soft notes drift, then fade away.
Silent chords through the night,
Dance of echoes, pure delight.

Each glance speaks, a tender sigh,
In stillness, dreams begin to fly.
Language of the heart unfolds,
A symphony, forever holds.

Through shadows deep, the stories weave,
In quietude, we believe.
Harmony in breaths we take,
Silent songs, love's sweet ache.

In the silence, worlds collide,
The unspoken, our silent guide.
Together in this melody,
Our hearts sing in perfect harmony.

Traces of Love in Shadows

Beneath the moon, soft shadows cling,
Fading echoes of love's spring.
Whispers linger, a gentle trace,
In the dark, we find our place.

Memories dance in twilight's glow,
Footprints left on paths we know.
The quiet speaks of hearts entwined,
In the shade, love redefined.

Each sigh of night, a calming breeze,
Holds our laughter, brings us peace.
In the silence, dreams unwind,
Traces of love, forever bind.

Beneath the stars, our secrets hum,
In shadows deep, we become one.
Through the night, our spirits soar,
Traces of love, forevermore.

Harmonies of the Heartbeat

In rhythm, hearts softly beat,
A melody that feels so sweet.
Two souls dancing, side by side,
In this harmony, we confide.

Each pulse a note, holding tight,
In the stillness of the night.
Vibrations weave a tender song,
Together where we both belong.

With every moment, love's refrain,
We're weathering through joy and pain.
In the quiet, a gentle spread,
Harmonies where our dreams are bred.

Through life's journey, hand in hand,
In perfect sync, we understand.
Beats entwined, a bond so dear,
Our hearts echo, always near.

A Tapestry of Gentle Memories

Threads of time, woven fine,
In the loom of love, we shine.
Colors blend, a radiant hue,
Gentle memories, crafted true.

Moments cherished, softly stitched,
In every tear, our joy enriched.
Woven whispers, secrets shared,
In the fabric, our hearts laid bare.

Patterns formed in laughter's song,
Through the years, we grow strong.
Each memory a cherished thread,
In the tapestry, we are wed.

As seasons change, the weave expands,
In life's embrace, we take our stands.
A masterpiece of love and grace,
Gentle memories, our sacred space.

The Unseen Gallery of Love

In shadows where soft whispers dwell,
Silent treasures, stories to tell.
Brush strokes of longing paint the night,
In colors unseen, hearts take flight.

Frames of laughter, echoes of pain,
Captured moments in joy and rain.
Every gaze a canvas of dreams,
An artful dance of love's sweet schemes.

In this space, we gently collide,
Hidden feelings, we cannot hide.
A gallery filled with our souls' grace,
In quiet corners, we find our place.

Melodies of the Hidden Heart

In the depths where shadows play,
A silent song begins to sway.
Notes of longing gently soar,
Echoes of love, forevermore.

Each heartbeat, a rhythm entwined,
A secret dance of souls combined.
In whispered winds, our passions call,
Melodies rise, we lose and fall.

Chords of laughter, sighs of bliss,
Every ache, a tender kiss.
In the quiet, our spirits meet,
In this harmony, love feels complete.

Illuminating the Unexpressed

In the dark where silence thrums,
A flicker of light softly comes.
Shadows dance upon the wall,
Illuminating hearts enthralled.

Every glance, a spark ignites,
Revealing truths through silent fights.
Words unspoken find their way,
In the glow of night and day.

A lantern held, we gently tread,
Through the whispers of what is said.
In the light, our secrets unfurl,
A tapestry woven in this world.

The Art of Vulnerable Viewing

Through transparent frames, we gaze inside,
Catch the truth that we often hide.
Brush strokes of fear, colors of trust,
In vulnerable moments, we learn to adjust.

Eyes wide open to scars that speak,
Every crack shows the strength we seek.
Within the ugly, the beauty thrives,
In fragile forms, true love survives.

An artist's heart in every glance,
In this rawness, we dare to dance.
In the art of seeing, we find release,
A vulnerable touch that brings us peace.

Whispers of the Soul's Light

In the silence where thoughts reside,
Gentle echoes of hope abide.
Flickers of warmth, soft and bright,
Guiding hearts to find their flight.

Whispers dance through the night air,
Carrying secrets, fragile as care.
With every breath, the spirit sings,
Embracing the joy that freedom brings.

Trust the voice that speaks within,
A tender song where dreams begin.
Through the shadows, let it soar,
Unlock the truth, forevermore.

In the Canvas of Emotion

Brushstrokes of love paint the sky,
Each color a tear, a heartfelt sigh.
Vivid moments captured in time,
Creating a rhythm, a silent rhyme.

A palette reflects the heart's bloom,
In shadows and light, it dances, finds room.
Emotions linger, vibrant and real,
On this canvas, the soul can heal.

Every hue tells a story untold,
In the depths of sorrow or joy so bold.
With each stroke, life finds its flow,
In the canvas, we learn to grow.

Shadows of Unspoken Dreams

In the twilight where secrets dwell,
Silent hopes whisper, a mystic spell.
Fragments of wishes float through the night,
Chasing the stars with shimmering light.

Shadows linger, yet so profound,
Carrying dreams that hope has found.
Beneath the surface, desires ignite,
Guided by whispers, they take flight.

Let the heart weave a tapestry fine,
Of shadows and light, interwoven design.
For in the silence, dreams take form,
Crafting a world where hearts stay warm.

Colors of a Beating Muse

A symphony of colors bursts awake,
With every heartbeat, new worlds we make.
Inspiration flows like rivers wide,
Carving paths where dreams can slide.

The muse whispers with chaotic grace,
Painting life at a vibrant pace.
Each stroke carries a story, a song,
Energizing spirits, where we belong.

Colors collide, a beautiful mess,
Creating visions, we dare to express.
In the beating of hearts, art comes alive,
Fueling the passion, helping us thrive.

The Inner Lenses

Through glassy eyes, we see the world,
Each hue and shade, a story swirled.
In prisms bright, our dreams take flight,
Within the heart, the truth ignites.

Reflections dance like shadows cast,
In silent whispers, echoes past.
A flicker of light, a fleeting glance,
Chronicles spun in a fleeting trance.

Layers unfold, the mind reveals,
A tapestry woven, the soul feels.
Perspectives shifting like autumn leaves,
In every gaze, a truth believes.

The lens is clear, the vision wide,
In every moment, love and pride.
Together we walk, a journey vast,
In the inner depths, our futures cast.

Reflections on Love's Canvas

Crimson strokes upon the night,
Soft whispers framed in tender light.
Every heartbeat, a brush so bold,
Stories of love quietly unfold.

Colors blend in sweet embrace,
Artistry blooms in sacred space.
With every glance, a painter's sigh,
Love's canvas speaks without goodbye.

Texture rich, and shadows play,
Moments captured, gone astray.
In silent vows, two souls collide,
Unseen forces dance and glide.

With vivid hues, our hearts align,
In every frame, your hand in mine.
Reflections gleam in bright array,
Forever cherished, come what may.

When Feelings Speak

In silence deep, emotions stir,
A quiet heart where secrets blur.
With every pulse, a truth conveyed,
Words unspoken, yet not delayed.

A gaze that lingers, soft and kind,
In every look, a fate entwined.
Unraveled threads of thought expressed,
The language of love, unconfessed.

When shadows whisper, hearts respond,
Connections thrive, a timeless bond.
The sweetest sound is not so loud,
In stillness found, we are enshrouded.

As feelings rise like tides at play,
Together we find the words to say.
In this moment, the world stands still,
When feelings speak, our souls fulfill.

Echoes of Untold Yearnings

In twilight's grip, a secret sigh,
The stars above, our only tie.
I search the night for dreams unspooled,\nIn every
shadow, hopes are fueled.

Whispers carried on the breeze,
Softly weaving through the trees.
Yearnings rise like morning mist,
In every pulse, a love unkissed.

Fleeting glances, moments lost,
In gentle waves, we pay the cost.
With every heartbeat, wishes bloom,
And in the silence, echoes loom.

Stories linger in the air,
Untold yearnings lay us bare.
Together we chase the fading light,
In echoes deep, we find our flight.

A Kaleidoscope of Kindness

In every smile, a light we share,
A gentle touch, a breath of air.
Through acts of grace, our hearts align,
A world reborn, where love will shine.

In whispered words, we find our peace,
A bond of caring that won't cease.
Together we rise, hand in hand,
Creating joy across the land.

The Depths of Longing

In shadows deep, my heart does ache,
For dreams of you, the path I take.
A silent wish upon the night,
For love that lingers out of sight.

With every breath, your name I breathe,
In distant stars, my soul believes.
Through weary days, I search your face,
In the quiet, I find my place.

Dreams Woven in Sentiment

In twilight's glow, our visions blend,
Each thread of hope, a message send.
With every heartbeat, dreams ignite,
In twilight's calm, we take our flight.

Through fields of thought, we wander free,
In woven tales of you and me.
Together we craft a future bright,
Embracing all that feels so right.

The Soft Lens of Affection

Through gentle eyes, the world we view,
A softer touch in all we do.
With every glance, a story told,
In warmth of heart, we mend the cold.

In tender moments, love will bloom,
A dance of light, dispelling gloom.
Each heartbeat echoes, pure and clear,
A symphony that draws us near.

Secrets Hidden in Stillness

In the hush of the twilight glow,
Whispers linger, soft and slow.
Beneath the veil of silent trees,
Hidden truths float on the breeze.

Shadows dance in the fading light,
Secrets kept from day and night.
Gentle breeze carries the sigh,
Of stories shared with the shy.

In stillness, the heart finds peace,
Wandering thoughts begin to cease.
Moments wrapped in tender grace,
Unfolding mysteries we chase.

From quiet corners of our mind,
The hidden gems we seek to find.
With every pause, a truth is told,
In silence, stories still unfold.

Radiance in the Quiet Moments

In the dawn's soft whispered light,
Gentle shadows take their flight.
Moments carved in gold so rare,
Radiate with tender care.

As the world slows down to breathe,
Calm surrounds like autumn leaves.
In the stillness, hearts ignite,
Finding warmth in pure delight.

Each quiet pause unveils the grace,
Of nature's soft and sweet embrace.
Every breath a chance to see,
The beauty held in silence free.

Embrace the calm, let worries fade,
In these moments, peace is laid.
The radiance of stillness shines,
In quiet paths, our spirit aligns.

The Melody of Unspoken Truths

In the space where silence weaves,
Feel the echo of heart's leaves.
Whispers linger in the air,
Melodies beyond compare.

Songs of longing, softly sound,
In the quiet, love is found.
Every glance, a story speaks,
In their depths, the silence seeks.

Unveiling dreams like morning dew,
Truths that linger, pure and true.
In the stillness, hearts align,
Creating rhythms, so divine.

Let the quiet sing its tune,
Beneath the sun and silver moon.
In the shadows, secrets thrive,
In their essence, we arrive.

Compassion's Color Palette

Brush the canvas with soft hues,
Paint the world with gentle views.
Each stroke whispers tales of hope,
In compassion, we learn to cope.

Colors blend, a stunning sight,
Vibrant shades, a beacon light.
In every heart, a story glows,
In every soul, a kindness flows.

With every act, a hue is born,
From loving deeds, compassion's worn.
We find strength in colors' grace,
Uniting all in warm embrace.

Let the palette shine and share,
A masterpiece beyond compare.
In every shade, a truth is found,
Compassion's beauty knows no bound.

The Soul's Reflection

In silence deep, the thoughts unfold,
Mirrors held, the truth is told.
Whispers soft in twilight's glow,
A canvas painted, heart in tow.

Beneath the stars, dreams take flight,
In shadows dance, the day to night.
Threads of hope weave through despair,
In every breath, the soul laid bare.

Waves of time, they ebb and flow,
Echoes past, in whispers, sow.
In stillness, find the light within,
A journey starts where all begins.

A gentle touch, the spirit's plea,
In depths of night, we seek to be.
Each moment lived, a lesson learned,
In every heart, the fire burns.

Glimmers in the Heart's Prism

In every glance, a spark ignites,
A dance of colors, pure delights.
Through laughter shared, through tears that fall,
Glimmers shine, we heed the call.

With every heartbeat, rhythms play,
A symphony in night and day.
Memories crafted with thread so fine,
A tapestry of love's design.

The softest words, like petals drift,
Each moment shared, a cherished gift.
In every sigh, in dreams embraced,
Hope's gentle glow, our lives are laced.

In solitude, we find the way,
The prism brightens, colors sway.
United souls, forever bound,
In every heart, true love is found.

Echoes of Emotion's Light

In shadows long, the whispers gleam,
Echoes linger, like a dream.
Through pain and joy, a path is paved,
In every scar, a strength engraved.

A flicker bright in darkest night,
The heart awakens, seeking light.
In every heartbeat, stories flow,
A river deep, emotions grow.

From silence born, the truths arise,
In gentle hues, the spirit flies.
With every tear, a tale unfolds,
In every warmth, a hand to hold.

The light we share, it guides the way,
Binding hearts in soft array.
Through echoes of this tender plight,
Together we rise, in love's delight.

Underneath the Veil of Sentiment

Beneath the veil where feelings dwell,
A hidden world, a silent spell.
In whispered dreams, our spirits roam,
Together here, we find our home.

The colors blend, in soft embrace,
Each heartbeat finds a timeless space.
Through fleeting glances, love ignites,
In tender words, the heart's delights.

In shadows deep, where secrets lie,
We weave our hopes, we learn to fly.
With every breath, a promise made,
In memories, our love displayed.

Underneath the stars, we'll stand,
In whispered wishes, hand in hand.
Through every moment, pure and sweet,
Our souls entwined, we remain complete.

Unraveling the Tapestry of Longing

Threads of dreams weave tight and bold,
Whispers of stories waiting to unfold.
Each color, a memory, vibrant and rare,
Yearning for touch, for someone to share.

Days pass slowly, shadows creep in,
Echoes of laughter, where do they begin?
Fingers trace patterns, a map of the heart,
Longing, a canvas, where love and art part.

In stillness, the silence wraps tight like a cloak,
Yearning for voices that once were bespoke.
An ache that lingers, like dusk in the sky,
Unraveling threads, they dance and sigh.

Yet hope persists in the dimmest of light,
Promising dawn after long winter's night.
With each small stitch, a promise is sewn,
In the tapestry crafted, I'm never alone.

Light Filtering Through Pulse and Vein

Softly it dances, that flickering gleam,
Merging with heartbeats, alive in a dream.
Golden reflections on skin, they play,
A rhythm of life in the dawn's gentle sway.

Veins coursing stories, a luminous trace,
Mapping the journeys, each time and place.
Glimmers of hope in the darkest of nights,
Threads of connection in soft, whispered lights.

Every heartbeat, a note in the air,
A symphony birthed from a lover's despair.
In the quiet, a pulse resonates wide,
Guiding the souls who will not be denied.

Filtered through moments, each breath a renewal,
Cascading warmth, our sacred retrieval.
Light as an echo, through flesh and through bone,
Together we pulsate, never alone.

Secrets Written on the Wind

Whispers in twilight, secrets set free,
Carried by breezes, as soft as can be.
Leaves rustle softly, a language profound,
In the hush of the evening, lost truths can be found.

Dancing through branches, they twist and they blend,
Words of the ages, both foe and friend.
A touch from the past, a hint of the now,
In each gentle gust, history bows.

Echoes of laughter from shores long ago,
Memories flicker with each ebb and flow.
Nature reveals what the heart cannot speak,
In the sigh of the air, it's connection we seek.

Breathe in the whispers, let them take flight,
Secrets surrendered to the cloak of the night.
For every soft sigh, a promise unfurled,
In the wind's gentle currents, we share our world.

Tides of Emotion's Spectrum

Waves crash and tumble, a vibrant display,
Colors of feeling in the light of the day.
Rushing and pulling, the heart's ebb and flow,
Riding the currents, both high and below.

Cyan of the joy, a sky wide and true,
Amber of hope, with a hue that is new.
Crimson of anger, a fire burning bright,
Each tide a reflection of day turning night.

Gentle pastels brush over the sand,
Soft whispers of love, like a touch of a hand.
Indigo sorrow, deep as the sea,
Shaping the landscape of what's yet to be.

In every emotion, a story is spun,
A tapestry woven in the setting sun.
Across the horizon, our colors collide,
In the tides of emotion, we flourish and glide.

Lenses of Warmth and Understanding

Through the lens of kindness, we see,
A world painted in hues of empathy.
Each smile a bridge, each hand a guide,
Together we walk, side by side.

In the warmth of sharing our tales,
Our hearts unveil what never fails.
Understanding blooms like spring's new birth,
Transforming shadows to radiant worth.

Even in silence, connections grow,
A gentle touch may speak the flow.
With each glance, a story unfurls,
Uniting the vastness of our worlds.

By wearing these lenses, we find our way,
In the tapestry woven through night and day.
With warmth in our hearts and minds open wide,
We'll cherish the journey, as life's true guide.

The Heart's Uncharted Territories

In the depths of the heart, secrets lie,
Untamed landscapes under the sky.
Each beat a compass, guiding the way,
Through valleys of echoes where shadows play.

With every tear shed, a river flows,
Mapping the pain that each soul knows.
Yet in the silence, joy takes its flight,
Filling the void with shimmering light.

Exploring the crevices, we hear the song,
A melody soft where we all belong.
In the heart's vast realm, we discover new art,
Expressing the beauty of each tender part.

As we navigate these mysterious lands,
Resilience blooms in our trembling hands.
The heart, a treasure, forever to roam,
In uncharted territories, we find our home.

Reflections on the Canvas of Life

Life is a canvas, colors collide,
Moments of chaos, where dreams abide.
Each brushstroke tells a story anew,
A masterpiece formed from experiences true.

Pain mixes with joy, a palette divine,
Shades of elation and sorrow entwine.
With every trial, a stroke darker made,
The light emerges in hues that won't fade.

In quiet corners, we find peace and grace,
Reflections of time etched on each face.
Every laughter, every sigh captured bright,
In this gallery, we celebrate the light.

As we paint our journey, let love define,
The vivid reflections on this canvas of mine.
Each layer a lesson, each shade a chance,
To embrace the beauty, and forever dance.

A Palette of Emotional Landscapes

In valleys low, emotions converge,
Where shadows linger and feelings surge.
Each hue a story, from deep to light,
Painting our spirits in day and night.

The sunlit yellows of laughter and cheer,
Contrast sharply with blues born of fear.
In the mix, greens of hope slowly rise,
Crafting a masterpiece before our eyes.

Misty grays whisper of loss and despair,
While vibrant reds ignite the passion we share.
These landscapes vast, shaped by our hands,
Creating a world where understanding stands.

With each brush dipped in love and care,
We paint our lives, and the truth laid bare.
In this palette of emotions, we grow,
Finding strength in the colors that flow.

The Symphony of Inner Sight

In silence, thoughts begin to swirl,
Melodies of dreams unfurl.
Each note a whisper, soft and clear,
The heart's true sound we long to hear.

A symphony of colors bright,
Illuminates the depths of night.
With every chord, a story grows,
Of hidden truths that no one knows.

Within the mind, a dance unfolds,
The beauty of a world untold.
In harmony, the soul takes flight,
Guided by the inner light.

Echoes of what we feel inside,
A melody we cannot hide.
With every breath, we find new grace,
The symphony in our embrace.

Visions Cast in Affection's Embrace

In gentle whispers, hearts collide,
Through tender dreams, we confide.
Each glance a promise, glowing bright,
In passion's dance, we take our flight.

Visions cast in softest light,
Unraveled threads of day and night.
With every touch, the world stands still,
In affection's warmth, we find our will.

Moments linger, sweet and rare,
In love's embrace, we shed our care.
A canvas painted with our sighs,
Reflections caught in lover's eyes.

Together woven, hearts entwined,
In dreams of you, our souls aligned.
With every heartbeat, futures weave,
In affection's glow, we believe.

Whispers of Love's Vision

In dreams we share, our secrets glide,
A silent bond that won't divide.
Whispers travel through the night,
Filling hearts with pure delight.

Each gaze a story yet to tell,
In every word, we know so well.
With gentle touch, the spirits soar,
In love's embrace, we seek for more.

The fleeting moments, soft and sweet,
In echoes soft, our hearts compete.
To paint the sky with shades of blue,
In whispers wrapped, I cherish you.

Across the dawn, our visions blend,
A promise made that will not end.
With every heartbeat, love ignites,
In whispered dreams, we claim the nights.

Shadows of a Tender Gaze

In shadows soft, where secrets hide,
A tender gaze opens wide.
A world revealed through eyes so deep,
In silence, we promise to keep.

Each fleeting glance, a silent vow,
Reflecting love's eternal now.
As twilight wraps the day in gold,
Our stories whisper, brave and bold.

With every heartbeat, moments freeze,
In gentle warmth, the soul finds ease.
A dance in shadows, hand in hand,
In tender sight, together stand.

The glow of love, a guiding star,
In shadows' arms, we've come so far.
Through every trial, we will chase,
The shadows cast by a tender gaze.

Reflections on Fragile Moments

In whispers soft, the shadows play,
Memories linger, then drift away.
Time holds secrets, both near and far,
Fleeting glimpses of who we are.

A tender glance, a sigh, a pause,
Life unfolds without a clause.
In fragile moments, truth will shine,
A fragile dance, both yours and mine.

Like petals falling from a bloom,
Each moment crafted in the loom.
We grasp the light, but shadows creep,
In silent depths, our sorrows seep.

Yet hope remains, a gentle stream,
Through dusky nights, we chase the dream.
In fragile moments, hearts ignite,
A spark of love, a guiding light.

The Map of Yearning Hearts

In every line, a story waits,
Drawn in silence, true as fates.
An atlas carved in whispered dreams,
A landscape painted in moonbeams.

With trembling hands, we trace each path,
Through joy and sorrow, love's sweet math.
In hidden corners, feelings grow,
A symphony of ebb and flow.

Stars like lanterns guide our way,
As yearning hearts dare to sway.
Unraveled maps of old and new,
A journey taken, bold and true.

Together we roam this quiet night,
In the map of longing, we find our light.
With every step, we grow more wise,
In the dance of hearts beneath the skies.

Visions Born from Laughter

In echoes bright, our laughter rings,
A melody that freedom brings.
With every giggle, joy takes flight,
A canvas splashed with colors bright.

The world unfolds in funny frames,
As playful spirits spark their flames.
Through silly tales and sparkling eyes,
We find the truth that never lies.

With whimsy's touch, we chase the sun,
In laughter shared, our hearts are one.
Each chuckle weaves a tapestry,
Of friendship pure, a symphony.

So let the moments dance and twirl,
In this vast, enchanting whirl.
Visions born from laughter's art,
Forever cherished in the heart.

Through the Prism of Emotion

Emotions swirl like colors bright,
In every heart, a different light.
Through laughter, sorrow, love, and fear,
We view the world, both far and near.

A prism shows what eyes may miss,
In shades of joy, in shades of bliss.
Each feeling crafted, a work of art,
Reflecting truths within the heart.

Through stormy skies, and gentle pleas,
We navigate with search for ease.
For in this spectrum, clear and vast,
We learn from futures and from pasts.

Each hue a lesson, bright and bold,
In stories shared, and tales retold.
Through the prism, the heart takes flight,
Guided by love, our truest light.

Shades of Love's Complexity

In shadows deep, we find our way,
Whispers of heart, in the light of day.
Colors blend, as laughter spills,
A tapestry woven, with all our wills.

The weight of silence, a comforting cloak,
Echoes of words, unspoken, bespoke.
Threads of joy, intertwined with pain,
Love blooms fiercely, through joy and strain.

Mirrored reflections in soulful glance,
Each heartbeat's rhythm, a sacred dance.
In tangled paths, we walk as one,
Underneath the same radiant sun.

Yet layers unfold, in time's embrace,
With every heartbeat, we find our place.
In shades of love, complex and true,
Forever entwined, just me and you.

The Language of Touch

Fingertips dance on skin so bare,
A silent promise, a breath of air.
In the quiet night, soft murmurs play,
Our bodies speak what words can't say.

A gentle caress, electric delight,
Skin on skin, we melt in the night.
The warmth of your gaze ignites a spark,
Illuminating shadows, chasing the dark.

In every embrace, emotions swell,
The language of touch, a secret spell.
In lingering hugs where time stands still,
We create a world that bends to our will.

In the space between heartbeats, we lay,
Bound by affection, come what may.
For within each touch, lies a story to find,
In this dance of flesh, our souls aligned.

Fables of the Beating Soul

In the heart's chambers, stories reside,
Of love that conquers, of pain that hides.
Fables spun from laughter and tears,
Unraveling gently through the years.

Each thump a tale, of joy or woe,
A rhythm that guides where passions flow.
In shadows cast by the moonlight's grace,
We find in each other, a sacred space.

Timeless adventures, together we weave,
Painting the world with colors believe.
Through trials faced, we stand as one,
With every heartbeat, our love's begun.

An echo of dreams, beneath the stars,
Fables of us, with all our scars.
In the book of life, our chapters fold,
A tale of the beating soul, forever told.

As Colors Fade, Love Remains

The sun dips low, casting shadows long,
Fleeting colors fade, but our song stays strong.
In the twilight glow, memories shine bright,
Guiding us gently into the night.

With every sunset, another begins,
A cycle of hues, where love never thins.
Time may wear, but we are steadfast,
In the heart's embrace, our moments last.

Through seasons we change, as days roll by,
Yet love whispers sweet under the vast sky.
In laughter's echo and tears that fall,
As colors fade, love conquers all.

So hand in hand, through storms, we'll walk,
In the silence shared, let our hearts talk.
For as oceans shift and stars may wane,
In the tapestry woven, love will remain.

Portraits of a Yearning Soul

In shadows cast by twilight's glow,
A whisper sings of dreams untold.
The heartache forms a silent plea,
For wings to soar, to be set free.

Through every crack in weary walls,
A glimpse of hope, a soft light calls.
Yet pain and joy entwine as one,
In the dance of dusk, a journey spun.

With every breath, the longing grows,
A brush of fate, where time bestows.
Each moment fleeting, rich, and rare,
A canvas etched with tender care.

So here I stand, with arms unlatched,
Seeking the dreams I long dispatched.
A yearning soul on pathways bright,
In search of love, in search of light.

The Pulse of Introspection

In silence deep, the mind expands,
Seeking truths with trembling hands.
Reflections swirl in whispered tones,
As echoes dance among the stones.

Each question forms a gentle weight,
As shadows loom, I contemplate.
A tapestry of thought unfolds,
With threads of fear and courage bold.

In solitude, the spirit roams,
Through hidden paths, it finds its homes.
A heartbeat sings, a calming sound,
Where peace resides, and hope is found.

The pulse of life within these roots,
Awake, alive, in sacred truths.
Through spiraled thoughts, I walk this way,
Embracing night, embracing day.

Veins of Aesthetic Dreams

In colors bright, my visions flow,
Like rivers weaving, soft and slow.
With every stroke, a story grows,
In threads of light where beauty glows.

The whispers of the dawn inspire,
A canvas painted, born from fire.
Each hue, a heartbeat, bold and free,
A testament to what can be.

In every brush, a pulse is found,
As art transcends the earthly ground.
Veins intertwine, both pain and grace,
In this pursuit, I find my place.

With dreams alive, I sculpt the night,
Imagining worlds bathed in light.
Through art, I cast my hopes and schemes,
A journey penned in aesthetic dreams.

Canvas of Compassion

Upon the canvas, love takes flight,
In strokes of kindness, pure and bright.
Each heart a hue in the grand design,
A masterpiece of souls entwined.

The gentle touch, a soft embrace,
In every corner, warmth finds grace.
A vibrant scene where tears can mend,
The healing art that we extend.

With open hands, we paint the world,
In colors deep, our spirits twirled.
Compassion flows like rivers wide,
A tapestry where hope resides.

Together we create the scene,
A canvas rich, where hearts convene.
With every act, a brush in hand,
We color life, we understand.

Inklings of Unsung Stories

In shadows where secrets dwell,
Whispers of time begin to swell.
Untold tales in silence weave,
Hope in darkness, we believe.

Ink on paper, dreams take flight,
Faded echoes, lost in night.
Each page turned, a life unfolds,
In every heart, a story holds.

Moments captured, glances shared,
Hearts unspoken, deeply cared.
In every sorrow, joy is sown,
Through unsung tales, we are known.

With every word, a spark ignites,
Revealing worlds in endless sights.
Inklings of stories wait in line,
To dance among the stars that shine.

Tints of Hope in Every Heartbeat

Every pulse, a silent prayer,
In shadows cast, we seek repair.
Colors brighten, fears decay,
In heartbeats, hope finds its way.

Gentle rhythms, soft and clear,
Promise whispers, drawing near.
Through the storm, a light will gleam,
Tints of hope in every dream.

Moments flicker, bright like stars,
Healing light through all our scars.
Every heartbeat keeps us strong,
In love's embrace, we still belong.

Let each breath inspire our fight,
Chasing shadows into light.
With every heartbeat, dreams impart,
The vibrant hues within the heart.

Melodies of Memory's Gaze

Songs of yesteryears arise,
In memory's arms, time defies.
Notes like whispers, soft and sweet,
In quiet corners, pasts repeat.

Echoes linger, feelings blend,
Through the ages, they transcend.
Each melody a fleeting trace,
In the heart, a sacred space.

When laughter dances, tears may flow,
In harmonies, our stories grow.
Every chord, a life embraced,
Melodies of memory traced.

With each refrain, the soul will sigh,
In rhythms lost, we learn to fly.
Music binds us, near and far,
In every note, a shining star.

The Embrace of Infinite Possibilities

In twilight's glow, dreams arise,
The unknown whispers, boldly flies.
With every choice, paths intertwine,
Embracing worlds where stars align.

Each moment cradles uncharted grace,
Endless journeys, each new face.
Beyond the limits, hearts expand,
In possibilities, we make our stand.

With courage sewn in every seam,
We step into the boundless dream.
Holding hands with fate so bright,
Together, we embrace the light.

Infinite dances await the brave,
In life's great ocean, we will wave.
With every heartbeat, chance will sing,
To the embrace of everything.

Gazing Beyond the Veil

In twilight's hush, the stars emerge,
Whispers of night begin to surge.
Eyes like lanterns, soft and bright,
Guiding souls through the silent night.

Beneath the moon's gentle embrace,
We wander far, in a timeless space.
Dreams unfold like petals wide,
Inviting wonder, where secrets hide.

Threads of fate entwine our fears,
Painting moments, we hold dear.
Gazing beyond the veil so thin,
Where love begins and shadows spin.

In cosmic dance, our spirits soar,
To realms unknown, we long for more.
With every heartbeat, we transcend,
In this journey, there's no end.

Heartstrings and Sunbeams

In a meadow where wildflowers bloom,
Two hearts collide, dispelling gloom.
Laughter echoes, bright and clear,
As sunbeams quiver, drawing near.

Fingers entwined, we dance with glee,
Each moment shared, sweet harmony.
The world of colors comes alive,
Where dreams ignite and spirits thrive.

With every glance, a story unfolds,
A tapestry of warmth that never grows cold.
Heartstrings strummed in joy's sweet air,
Binding us close, beyond compare.

As twilight descends, we chase the light,
Each sunset, a promise, holding tight.
In whispered vows beneath the trees,
Love's gentle breath brings us to ease.

The Silent Language of Affection

In every touch, a story flows,
A silent language only we know.
Eyes exchange what words can't say,
In brief, sweet moments, we find our way.

Gentle smiles that bridge the space,
Where laughter lingers in our embrace.
The warmth of knowing, hearts align,
An unspoken bond, tender and divine.

Through shadows cast, we seek the light,
In quiet corners, love takes flight.
No need for words, just presence strong,
In the silent dance, we both belong.

Time may pause as we draw near,
In every heartbeat, I hold you dear.
This sacred truth, we'll always share,
In silent whispers, love's sweet air.

Visions Born from Tenderness

In the cradle of dreams, we softly drift,
Woven in whispers, a precious gift.
Each vision born from tender care,
Igniting hope in the cool night air.

With every heartbeat, the world awakes,
Painting futures, as daylight breaks.
Gentle moments, we keep in trust,
Fleeting glimpses of love's pure thrust.

Through azure skies and gardens lush,
We roam with purpose, in a golden hush.
Hand in hand, we bravely tread,
Where visions flourish, no tears shed.

In the tapestry of life we weave,
Amidst the struggles, we still believe.
Visions born from tenderness bloom,
Lighting the path through every room.